How To Draw Fortnite For Kids: 3 Books In 1: Learn How to Draw Your Favorite Fortnite Characters

By: Andrew Howell

D1711893

Table Of Conents:

How To Draw Fornite For Kids: 40 Heroes

BASE EPIC

Draw his head with ears, rather long chin and hairstyle.

Continue with his neck, body and arms.

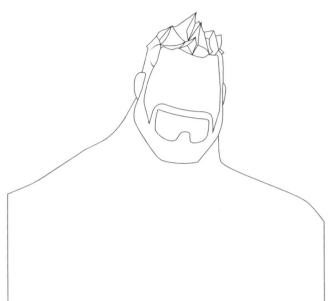

Draw eyes, eyebrows, nose and lips.

BASE EPIC

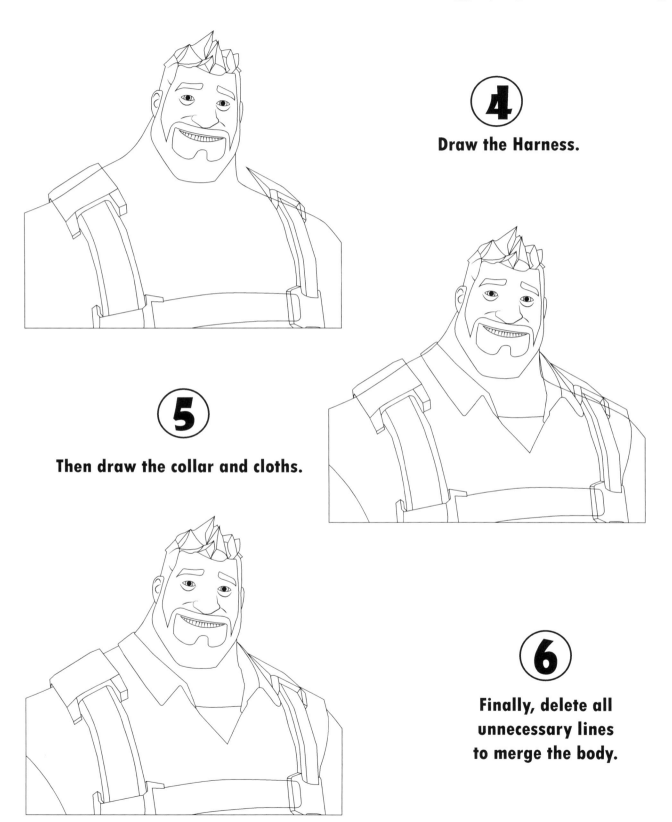

4

Draw the Harness.

5

Then draw the collar and cloths.

6

Finally, delete all unnecessary lines to merge the body.

GUNBLAZER EPIC

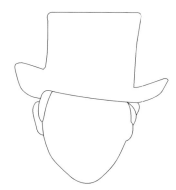

Draw his head with ears, rather long chin and hat.

Continue with his neck, arms.

Draw eyes, eyebrows, nose, lips, sunglass and the left lace.

GUNBLAZER EPIC

 4

Draw the other lace
and jacket with large collar.

 5

Then draw gas mask.

 6

Finally, delete all unnecessary lines
to merge the body.

BLUESTREAK ASSASSIN KEN

Draw his head with ears, rather long chin and spicky hairstyle.

Continue with his neck and arms.

Draw eyes, eyebrows, nose, lips and french beard.

BLUESTREAK ASSASSIN KEN

 Draw his scraf and ninja dress collar.

 Then draw the baldric and shoulder shield.

 Finally, delete all unnecessary lines to merge the body.

BRAWLER UNCOMMON

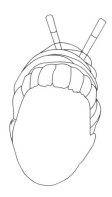

 1

Draw her head with
ears, rather long chin
and hairstyle with the stick.

 2

Continue with her neck, arms
and a line for chest.

 3

Draw eyes, eyebrows,
nose, lips, and ear ring.

BRAWLER UNCOMMON

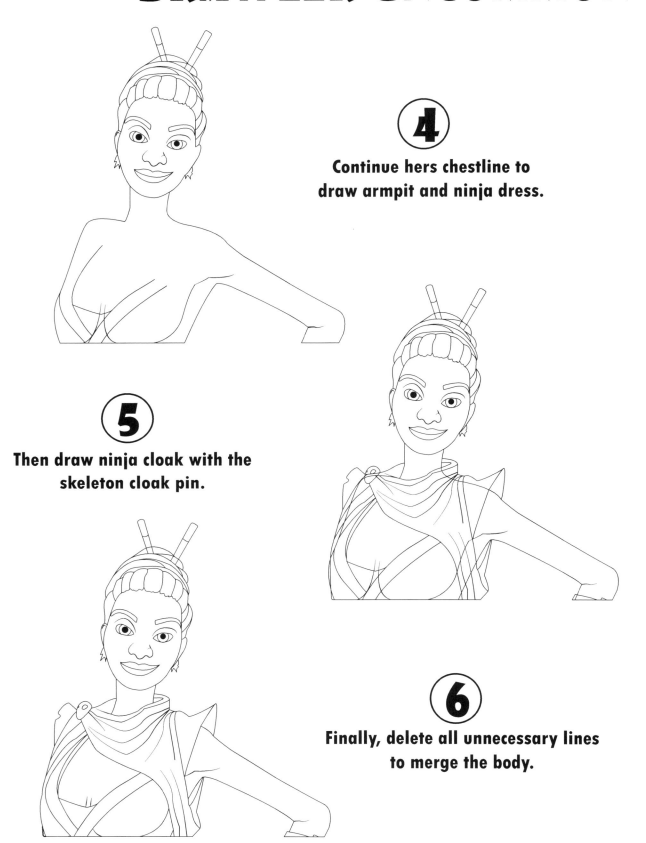

4 Continue hers chestline to draw armpit and ninja dress.

5 Then draw ninja cloak with the skeleton cloak pin.

6 Finally, delete all unnecessary lines to merge the body.

BULLET STORM JONESY

1

Draw his head with
googles shape, rather long chin
and spicky hairstyle.

2

Continue with his neck and arms.

3

Draw goggles, nose and lips.
Also the laces and baldric.

BULLET STORM JONESY

Draw the other lace, armband and design on the both arm.

Then draw lines on the body, dog tags and scarf.

Finally, delete all unnecessary lines to merge the body.

CENTURION HAWK

Draw his head with ears, rather long chin and hairstyle.

Continue with his neck and arms.

Draw eyes, eyebrows, nose, lips, mustache and beard. Also the lace and baldric.

CENTURION HAWK

4

Draw the other lace, armband and tattoo on the right arm.

5

Then draw dog tags and scarf.

6

Finally, delete all unnecessary lines to merge the body.

CENTURION LEGENDARY

**Draw her head with
ears, rather long chin
and hairstyle.**

**Continue with her neck, arms
and a line for chest**

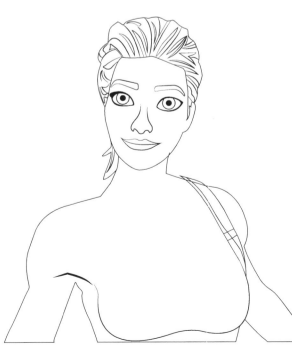

**Draw eyes, eyebrows, nose and lips.
Continue hers chestline to
draw armpit and lace.**

CENTURION LEGENDARY

4 Draw the other lace and armband.

5 Then draw dog tags and collar.

6 Finally, delete all unnecessary lines to merge the body.

CHROMIUM RAMIREZ

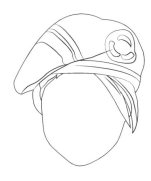

**Draw her head with
ears, rather long chin
and hairstyle.**

**Continue with her neck, arms
and a line for chest**

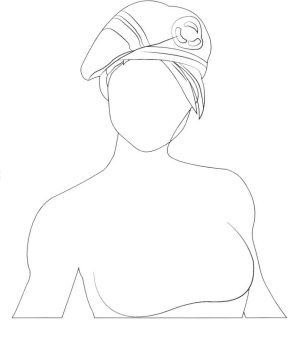

**Draw Googles, eyebrows, nose and lips.
Continue hers chestline to
draw armpit and lace.**

CHROMIUM RAMIREZ

Draw the other lace and armband.

Then draw the collar and lines
on the neck and left arm.

Finally, delete all unnecessary lines
to merge the body.

COMMANDO EPIC

Draw his head with ears, rather long chin and hairstyle.

Continue with his neck and arms.

Draw eyes, eyebrows, nose, lips, mustache and beard. Also the lace and baldric.

COMMANDO EPIC

Draw the other lace, armband and tattoo on the right arm.

Then draw dog tags, scarf and vest.

Finally, delete all unnecessary lines to merge the body.

DEADLY BLADE CRASH

Draw her head with ears, rather long chin and spicky hairstyle.

Continue with her neck, arms and a line for chest.

Draw eyes, eyebrows, nose, and lips.

DEADLY BLADE CRASH

Continue hers chestline to draw armpit and arm Gauntlets.

Then draw ninja dress and ninja cloak with the skeleton cloak pin.

Finally, delete all unnecessary lines to merge the body.

DEADLY BLADE LEGENDARY

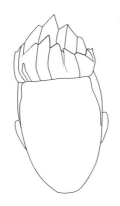

Draw his head with ears, rather long chin and spicy hairstyle.

Continue with his neck and arms.

Draw eyes, eyebrows, nose, lips and french beard.

DEADLY BLADE LEGENDARY

Draw his scraf and ninja
dress collar.

Then draw the baldric and
shoulder shield.

Finally, delete all unnecessary lines
to merge the body.

DOUBLE AGENT EVELYNN

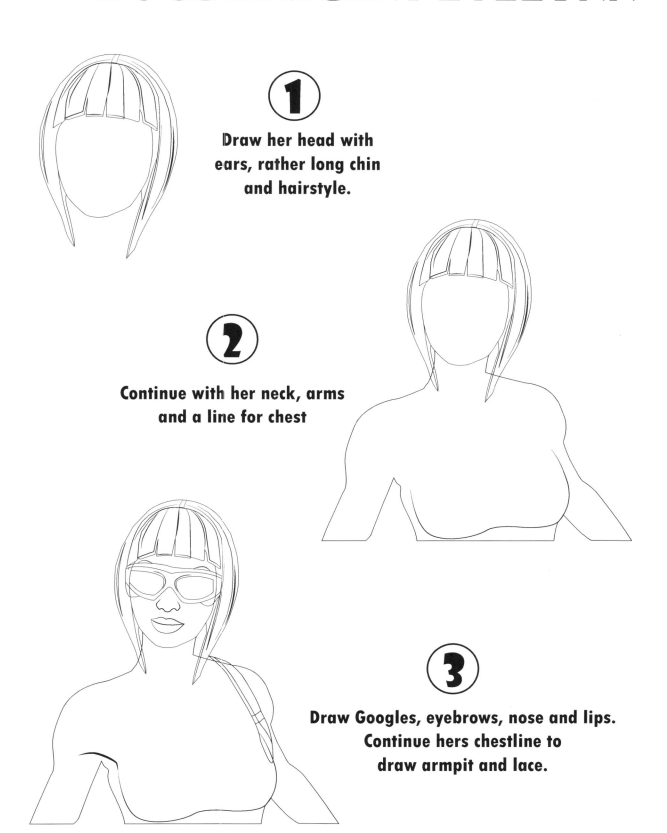

1

Draw her head with ears, rather long chin and hairstyle.

2

Continue with her neck, arms and a line for chest

3

Draw Googles, eyebrows, nose and lips. Continue hers chestline to draw armpit and lace.

DOUBLE AGENT EVELYNN

4 Draw the other lace and armband.

5 Then draw the collar and lines on the neck and left arm.

6 Finally, delete all unnecessary lines to merge the body.

DOUBLE AGENT VAUGHN

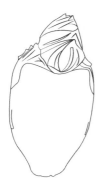

1

Draw his head with ears, rather long chin and spikey hairstyle.

2

Continue with his neck and arms.

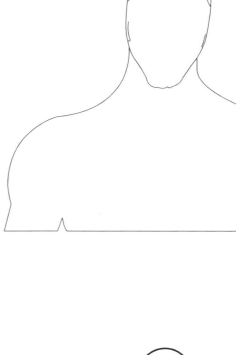

3

Draw eyes, eyebrows, nose, lips, mustache and beard. Also the lace and baldric.

DOUBLE AGENT VAUGHN

Draw the other lace, armband and tattoo on the right arm.

Then draw dog tags, scarf and vest.

Finally, delete all unnecessary lines to merge the body.

ENERGY THIEF MARI RARE

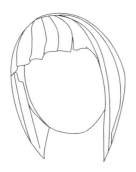

Draw her head with ears, rather long chin and hairstyle.

Continue with her neck, arms and a line for chest

Draw eyes, eyebrows, nose, and lips.

ENERGY THIEF MARI RARE

Continue hers chestline to draw armpit and arm Gauntlets.

Then draw ninja dress and ninja cloak with the skeleton cloak pin.

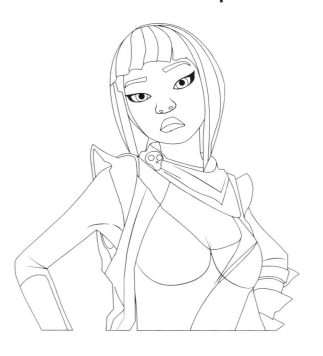

Finally, delete all unnecessary lines to merge the body.

ENFORCER EPIC

Draw his head with ears, rather long chin and spicy hairstyle.

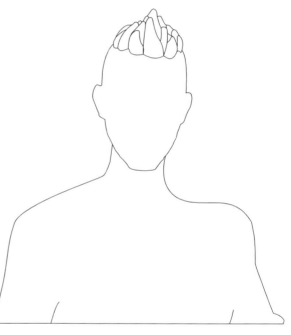

Continue with his neck, arms.

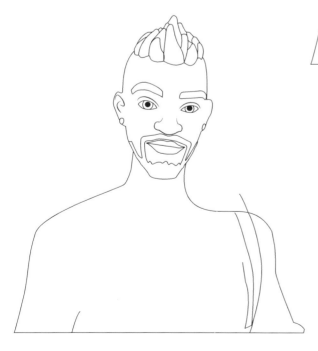

Draw eyes, eyebrows, nose, lips and left lace.

ENFORCER EPIC

**Draw the other lace
and jacket with large collar.**

Then draw gas mask.

**Finally, delete all unnecessary lines
to merge the body.**

EXPLOSIVE ASSASSIN KEN

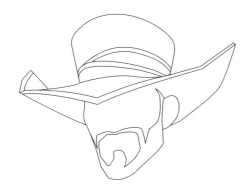

Draw his head with ears, rather long chin and hat.

Continue with his neck and arms.

Draw eyes, eyebrows, nose, lips and french beard.

EXPLOSIVE ASSASSIN KEN

Draw his scraf and ninja dress collar.

Then draw the baldric and shoulder shield.

Finally, delete all unnecessary lines to merge the body.

FLASH AC

 1

Draw his head with ears, rather long chin and spicky hairstyle.

 2

Continue with his neck, arms.

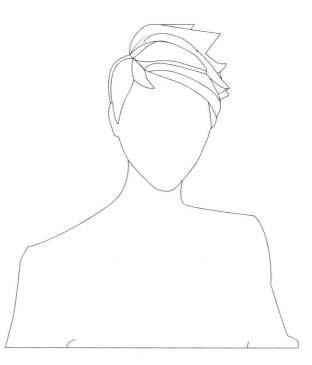

 3

Draw eyes, eyebrows, nose, lips and left lace.

FLASH AC

Draw the other lace and jacket with large collar.

Then draw gas mask.

Finally, delete all unnecessary lines to merge the body.

GUARDIAN EPIC

Draw his head with ears, rather long chin and hairstyle.

Continue with his neck, body and arms.

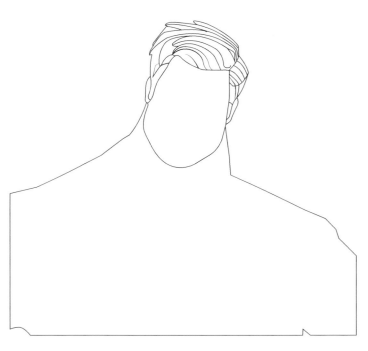

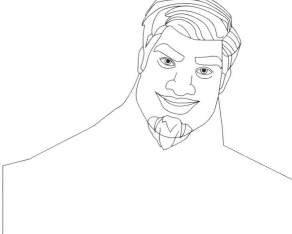

Draw eyes, eyebrows, nose and lips.

GUARDIAN EPIC

4 Draw the Harness.

5 Then draw the collar and cloths.

6 Finally, delete all unnecessary lines to merge the body.

GUNBLAZER EPIC

Draw his head with ears, rather long chin and spicky hairstyle.

Continue with his neck, arms.

Draw eyes, eyebrows, nose, lips, mark around the eye, and left lace.

GUNBLAZER EPIC

Draw the other lace and jacket with large collar.

Then draw gas mask.

Finally, delete all unnecessary lines to merge the body.

HUNTRESS

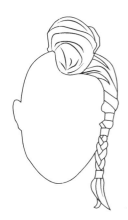

 Draw her head with ears, rather long chin and hairstyle.

 Continue with her neck, arms and a line for chest

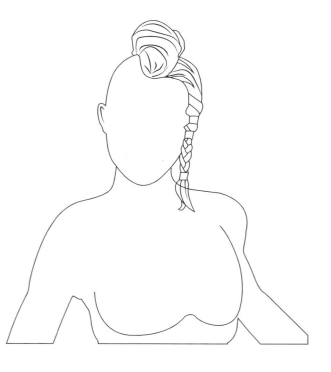

 Draw eyes, eyebrows, ear ring nose and lips. Continue her chestline to draw armpit and lace.

HUNTRESS

Draw the other lace, arm shield and shoulder guard.

Then draw body shield and collar.

Finally, delete all unnecessary lines to merge the body.

JADE ASSASSIN SARAH

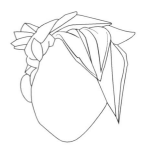

Draw her head with ears, rather long chin and spicky hairstyle.

Continue with her neck, arms and a line for chest.

Draw eyes, eyebrows, nose, lips and ear ring.

JADE ASSASSIN SARAH

 4

Continue her chestline to
draw armpit and arm Gauntlets.

 5

Then draw ninja dress and
ninja cloak with the
skeleton cloak pin.

 6

Finally, delete all unnecessary lines
to merge the body.

MACHINIST HARPER

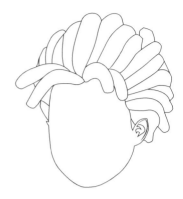

Draw her head with
ears, rather long chin
and hairstyle.

Continue with her neck, arms
and a line for chest

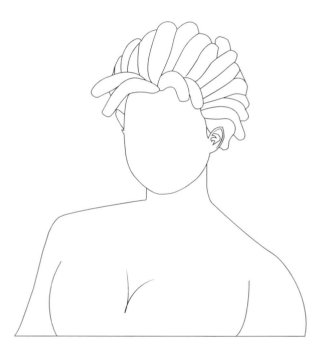

DDraw eyes, eyebrows, nose, and lips.
Continue her earring and tattoo on
the face.

MACHINIST HARPER

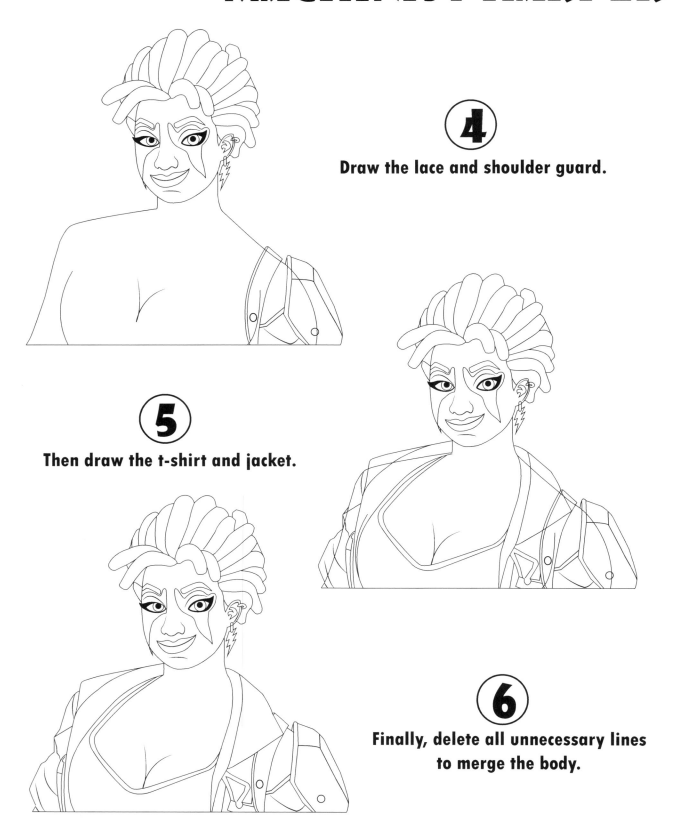

4 Draw the lace and shoulder guard.

5 Then draw the t-shirt and jacket.

6 Finally, delete all unnecessary lines to merge the body.

MASTER GRENADII

Draw her head with
ears, rather long chin
and hairstyle.

Continue with her neck, arms
and a line for chest

Draw eyes, eyebrows, nose and lips.
Continue her chestline to
draw armpit and lace.

MASTER GRENADIER

Draw the other lace and armband.

Then draw dog tags and collar.

6

Finally, delete all unnecessary lines
to merge the body.

PATHFINDER EPIC

Draw her head with ears, rather long chin and spiky hairstyle.

Continue with her neck, arms and chestline.

Draw eyes, eyebrows, nose, lips and mark around the eyes

PATHFINDER EPIC

Draw the jacket with long collar.

Then draw the scraf

Finally, delete all unnecessary lines to merge the body.

POWER BASE EPIC

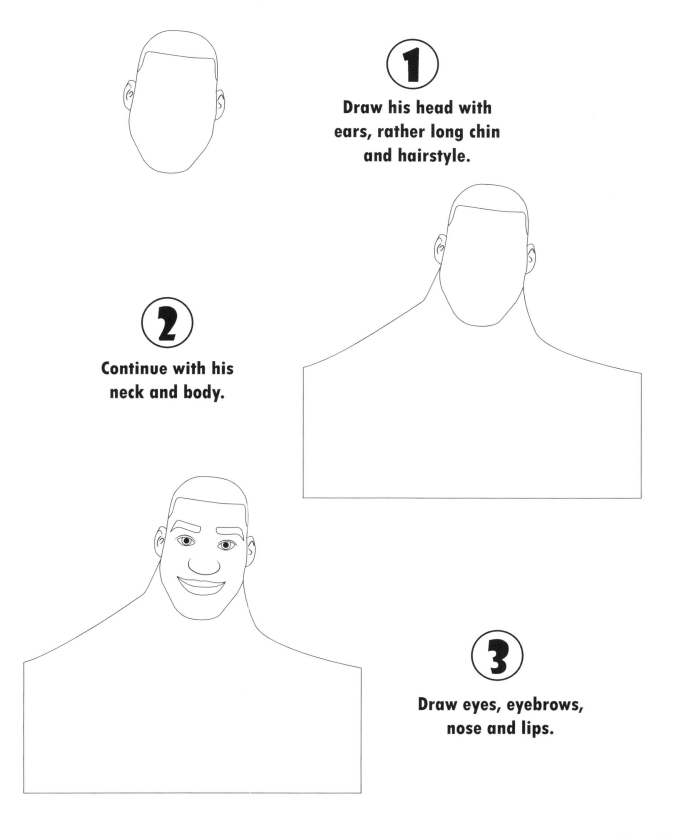

1 Draw his head with ears, rather long chin and hairstyle.

2 Continue with his neck and body.

3 Draw eyes, eyebrows, nose and lips.

POWER BASE EPIC

4 Draw the Harness.

5 Then draw the collar and cloths.

6 Finally, delete all unnecessary lines to merge the body.

RECON SCOUT EPIC

 1

**Draw her head with
ears, rather long chin
and spicky hairstyle.**

 2

**Continue with her neck,
arms and chestline.**

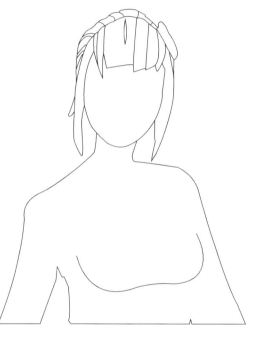

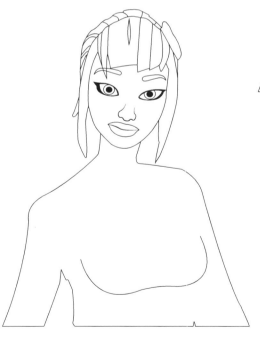

 3

**Draw eyes, eyebrows,
nose, and lips.**

RECON SCOUT EPIC

Draw the jacket with long collar and lace.

Then draw the scraf

Finally, delete all unnecessary lines to merge the body.

RESCUE TROOPER HAVOC

Draw his head with
the mask shape.

Continue with his neck and arms.

Draw eyes, eyebrows, mask.
Also the left side lace.

RESCUE TROOPER HAVOC

④

Draw the other lace and baldric.

⑤

Then draw the collar and zip on the chest.

⑥

Finally, delete all unnecessary lines to merge the body.

RIOT CONTROL HAZARD

Draw his head with ears, rather long chin and hairstyle.

Continue with his neck, body and arms.

Draw eyes, eyebrows, nose and lips.

RIOT CONTROL HAZARD

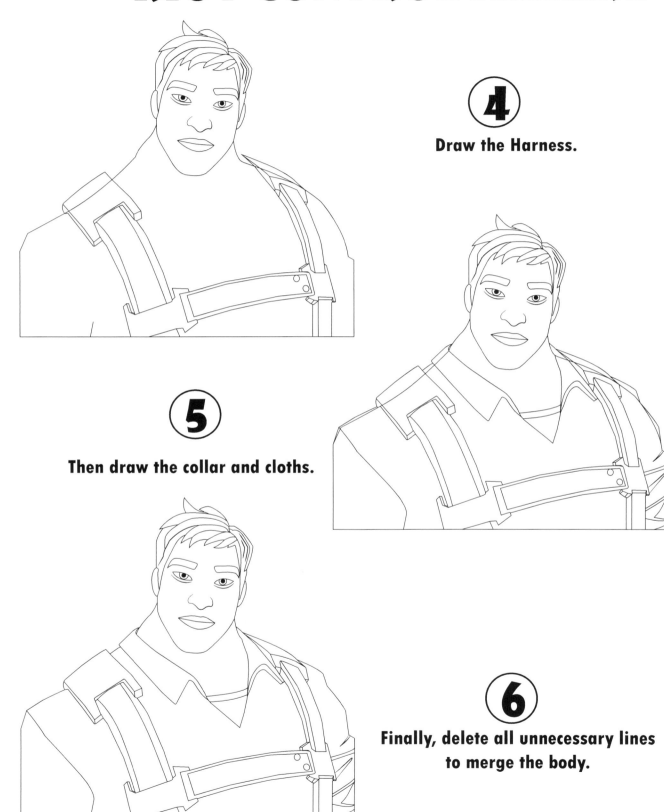

4 Draw the Harness.

5 Then draw the collar and cloths.

6 Finally, delete all unnecessary lines to merge the body.

RIOT CONTROL IZZA

Draw her head with ears, rather long chin and hairstyle.

Continue with her neck, arms and a line for chest.

Draw eyes, eyebrows, nose and lips. Continue hers chestline to draw the lace.

RIOT CONTROL IZZA

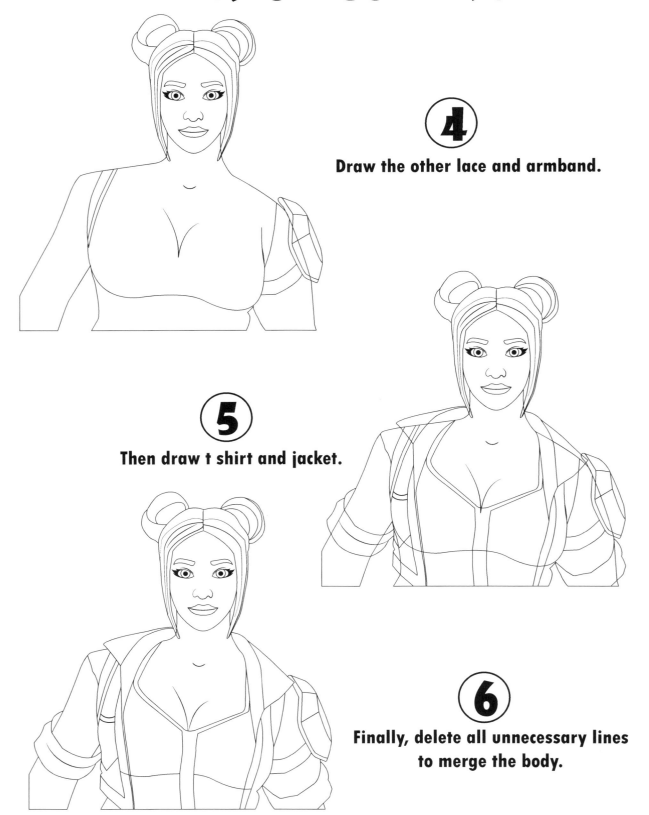

4

Draw the other lace and armband.

5

Then draw t shirt and jacket.

6

Finally, delete all unnecessary lines to merge the body.

SENTINEL EPIC

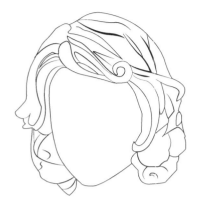

Draw her head with
ears, rather long chin
and hairstyle.

Continue with her neck, arms
and a line for chest.

Draw eyes, eyebrows, nose and lips.
Continue her chestline and lace.

SENTINEL EPIC

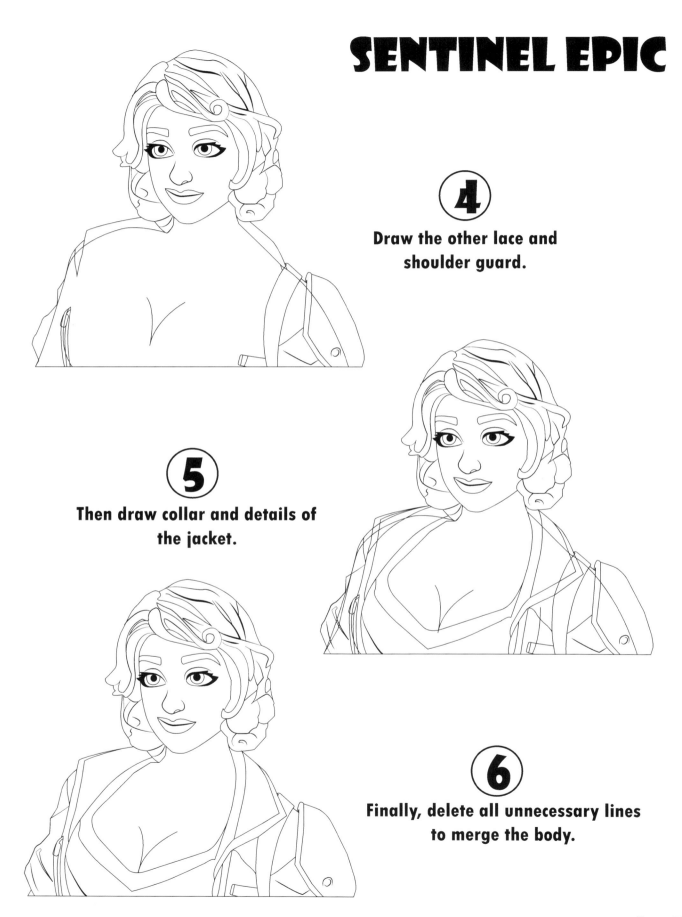

4 Draw the other lace and shoulder guard.

5 Then draw collar and details of the jacket.

6 Finally, delete all unnecessary lines to merge the body.

SERGEANT LEGENDARY

Draw his head with
ears, rather long chin
and hairstyle.

Continue with his neck and arms.

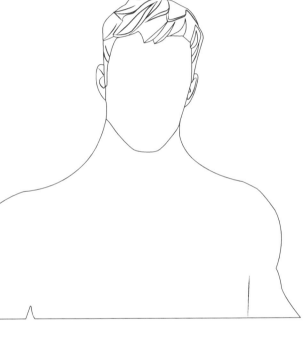

Draw eyes, eyebrows, nose and lips.
Also the laces and baldric.

SERGEANT LEGENDARY

4

Draw the other lace, armband and tattoo on the right arm.

5

Then draw dog tags and scarf.

6

Finally, delete all unnecessary lines to merge the body.

SHOCK GUNNER BUZZ

Draw her head with ears, rather long chin and spicky hairstyle.

Continue with her neck, arms and chestline.

Draw eyes, eyebrows, nose, and lips.

SHOCK GUNNER BUZZ

Draw the jacket with long collar and lace.

Then draw the scraf

Finally, delete all unnecessary lines to merge the body.

SKIRMISHER EPIC

**Draw his head with
ears, rather long chin
and spicky hairstyle.**

Continue with his neck and arms.

**Draw eyes, eyebrows, nose,
lips and french beard.**

SKIRMISHER EPIC

Draw his scraf and ninja dress collar.

Then draw the baldric and shoulder shield.

Finally, delete all unnecessary lines to merge the body.

SPECIAL FORCES RARE

Draw her head with ears, rather long chin and spiky hairstyle.

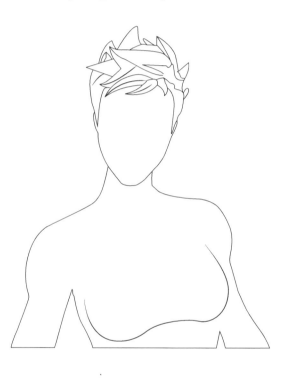

Continue with her neck, arms and a line for chest.

Draw eyes, eyebrows, nose and lips. Continue hers chestline to draw armpit and lace.

SPECIAL FORCES RARE

Draw the other lace and armband.

Then draw dog tags.

**Finally, delete all unnecessary lines
to merge the body.**

STEEL WOOL SYD

Draw his head with ears, rather long chin and hairstyle.

Continue with his neck and arms.

Draw sunglass, eyebrows, nose, lips, mustache. Also the left side lace.

STEEL WOOL SYD

4

Draw the other lace and locket.

5

Then draw the clothes.

6

Finally, delete all unnecessary lines
to merge the body.

TANK UNCOMMON

Draw her head with, rather long chin and hairstyle.

Continue with her neck, arm, shape of body and a line for chest

Draw eyes, eyebrows, nose and lips. Then draw the lace.

TANK UNCOMMON

4 Draw the other lace and shoulder guard.

5 Then draw the collar and clothes.

6 Finally, delete all unnecessary lines to merge the body.

THE CLOAKED STAR

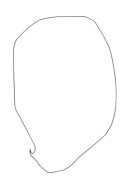

Draw his head and long chin.

Continue with his neck and arms.

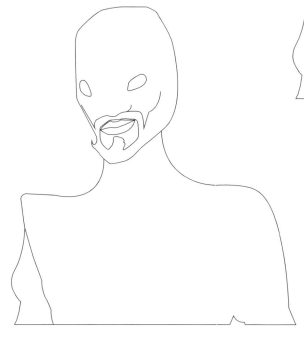

**Draw mask, eyes, nose,
lips and french beard.**

THE CLOAKED STAR

Draw his ninja dress, scraf, hoodie and long collar.

Then draw the baldric and shoulder shield.

Finally, delete all unnecessary lines to merge the body.

TRAILBLAZER EPIC

Draw her head with ears, rather long chin and spiky hairstyle.

Continue with her neck, arms and chestline.

Draw eyes, eyebrows, nose, and lips.

TRAILBLAZER EPIC

Draw the jacket with long collar and lace.

Then draw the scraf

Finally, delete all unnecessary lines to merge the body.

URBAN ASSAULT E'

**Draw her head with
ears, rather long chin
and hairstyle.**

**Continue with her neck, arms
and a line for chest.**

**Draw eyes, eyebrows, nose and lips.
Continue her chestline to
draw armpit and lace.**

URBAN ASSAULT EPIC

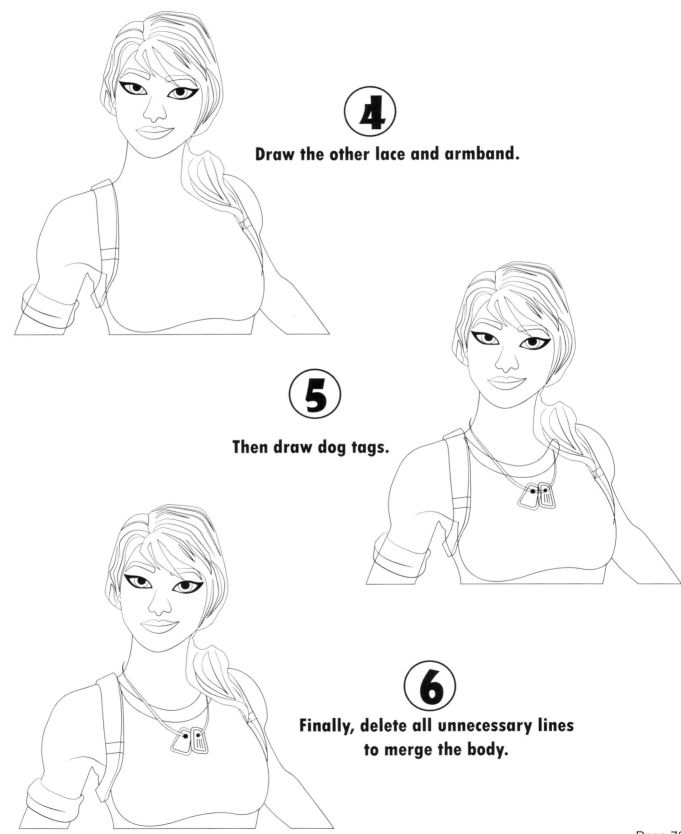

④ Draw the other lace and armband.

⑤ Then draw dog tags.

⑥ Finally, delete all unnecessary lines to merge the body.

WARRIOR WILDCAT

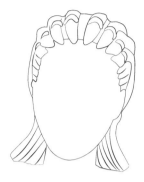

Draw her head with
ears, rather long chin
and hairstyle.

Continue with her neck, arms
and a line for chest

Draw eyes, eyebrows, nose and lips.
Continue hers chestline to
draw armpit and lace.

WARRIOR WILDCAT

4 Draw the other lace and armband.

5 Then draw the blade and shield on her back, collar.

6 Finally, delete all unnecessary lines to merge the body.

How To Draw Fortnite For Kids: Survivors

ADVENTUROUS SURVIVOR FEMALE 2

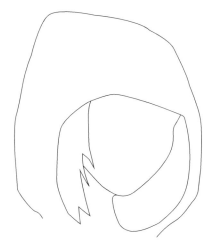

Draw the shape of
her head with hood and hair.

Continue with her hood,
Solder and details of the hair.

Draw eyes, eyebrows, nose,
ear and lips.

82

ADVENTUROUS SURVIVOR FEMALE 2

4

Draw her t-shirt with collar
and necklace.

5

Finally, delete all unnecessary lines
to merge the body.

ADVENTUROUS SURVIVOR FEMALE 3

1 Draw the shape of her head with cap and hairstyle.

2 Continue with her neck, Solder and details of the hair and chest line.

3 Draw eyes, eyebrows, nose, ear and lips.

84

ADVENTUROUS SURVIVOR FEMALE 3

4

Draw her dress, ear ring and necklace.

5

Finally, delete all unnecessary lines to merge the body.

ADVENTUROUS SURVIVOR MALE 3

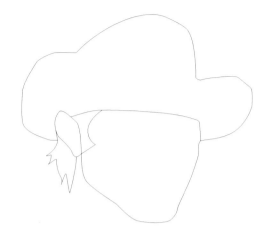

**Draw the shape of
his head with cap and hair.**

**Continue with his neck,
Solder and details of cap and hair.**

**Draw eyes, eyebrows, nose,
ear and lips.**

86

ADVENTUROUS SURVIVOR MALE 3

4

Draw his shirt with collar.

5

Finally, delete all unnecessary lines
to merge the body.

ANALYTICAL SURVIVOR FEMALE 1

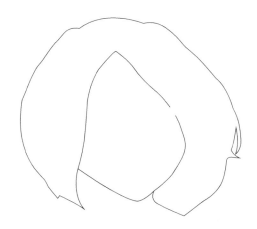

Draw the shape of her head with hairstyle.

Continue with her neck, arms, fingers and details line for hair.

Draw eyes, eyebrows, nose and lips.

ANALYTICAL SURVIVOR FEMALE 1

4 Draw her dress with collar.

5 Finally, delete all unnecessary lines to merge the body.

ANALYTICAL SURVIVOR FEMALE 2

1 Draw the shape of her head with hairstyle.

2 Continue with her neck, arms and details line for hair.

3 Draw eyes, eyebrows, nose and lips. Draw hers armpit and braslate.

ANALYTICAL SURVIVOR FEMALE 2

4

Draw her dress and lace.

5

Finally, delete all unnecessary lines
to merge the body.

91

COMPETITIVE SURVIVOR FEMALE 2

 1

**Draw the shape of
her head with the hair.**

2

**Continue with her neck,
Solder and details of the hair.**

 3

**Draw eyes, eyebrows, nose,
ear and lips.**

COMPETITIVE SURVIVOR FEMALE 2

Draw her dress with collar.

Draw her ear ring and necklace.

Finally, delete all unnecessary lines to merge the body.

COMPETITIVE SURVIVOR MALE 2

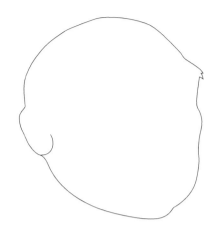

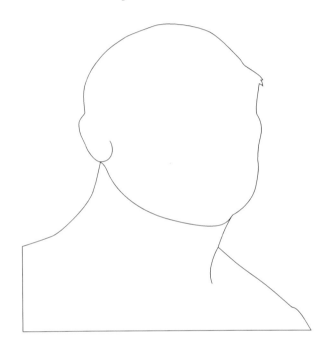

1

Draw the shape of his head.

2

Continue with his neck, Solder.

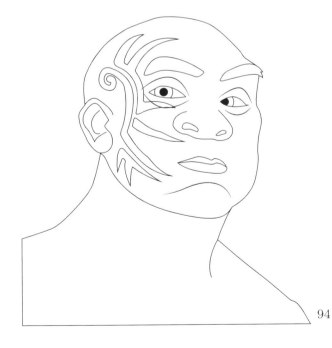

3

Draw eyes, eyebrows, nose,
ear, lips and tattoo.

94

COMPETITIVE SURVIVOR MALE 2

4

Draw his shirt with collar.

5

Finally, delete all unnecessary lines to merge the body.

COOPERATIVE SURVIVOR FEMALE 1

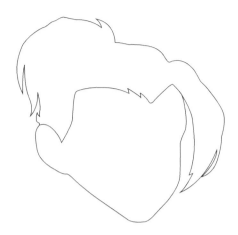

Draw the shape of her head with hair.

Continue with her neck, solder. Draw detail lines for the hair.

Draw eyes, eyebrows, nose, ear and lips.

96

COOPERATIVE SURVIVOR FEMALE 1

4

Draw her dress and collar.

5

Finally, delete all unnecessary lines to merge the body.

97

COOPERATIVE SURVIVOR FEMALE 2

Draw the shape of
his head with cap and hair.

Continue with his neck, hand,
Solder and details of the hair.

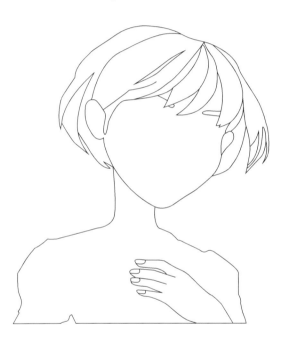

Draw eyes, eyebrows, nose,
ear and lips.

COOPERATIVE SURVIVOR FEMALE 2

Draw her dress.

Draw her necklace and bracelet.

5

Finally, delete all unnecessary lines to merge the body.

99

COOPERATIVE SURVIVOR MALE 2

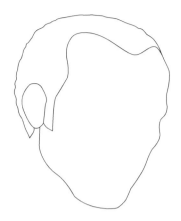

**Draw the shape of
his head with hairstyle.**

Continue with his neck and solders.

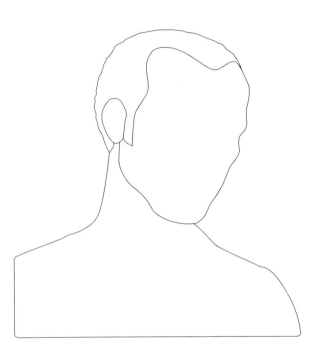

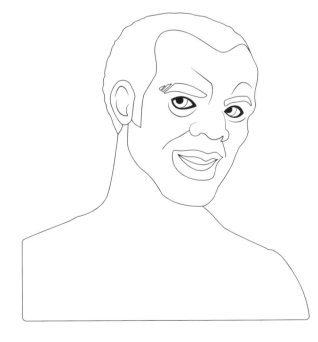

Draw eyes, eyebrows, nose, ear and lips.

100

COOPERATIVE SURVIVOR MALE 2

4

Draw his dress with details.

5

Finally, delete all unnecessary lines
to merge the body.

CURIOUS SURVIVOR FEMALE 1

1

Draw the shape of
her head with hair.

2

Continue with his neck,
Solder and details of the hair.

3

Draw eyes, eyebrows, nose,
ear and lips.

CURIOUS SURVIVOR FEMALE 1

4

Draw his hoode with collar,
ear ring and lace.

5

Finally, delete all unnecessary lines
to merge the body.

CURIOUS SURVIVOR MALE 1

Draw the shape of his head with hairstyle.

Continue with his neck, Solder and details hair.

Draw nose and lips.

CURIOUS SURVIVOR MALE 1

4 Draw his shirt with collar.

5 Finally, delete all unnecessary lines to merge the body.

DEPENDABLE SURVIVOR FEMALE 1

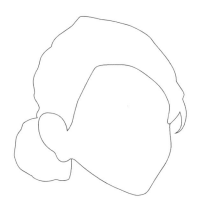

Draw the shape of her head with helmet.

Continue with her neck, solder. Draw lines for hair and details of the helmet.

Draw eyes, eyebrows, nose, ear and lips.

DEPENDABLE SURVIVOR FEMALE 1

4

Draw her dress collar.

5

Finally, delete all unnecessary lines
to merge the body.

DEPENDABLE SURVIVOR FEMALE 2

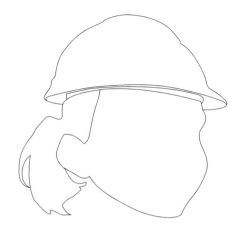

Draw the shape of
her head with helmet.

Continue with her neck, solder.
Draw lines for hair and details
of the helmet.

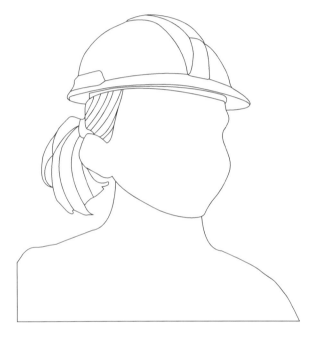

Draw eyes, eyebrows, nose,
ear and lips.

DEPENDABLE SURVIVOR FEMALE 2

(4)

Draw her Jacket with collar.

(5)

Finally, delete all unnecessary lines
to merge the body.

109

DEPENDABLE SURVIVOR MALE 3

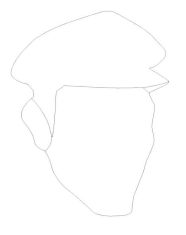

Draw the shape of his head with cap.

Continue with her neck, arms and details line for cap.

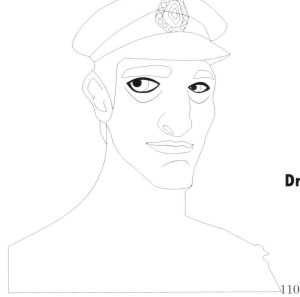

Draw eyes, eyebrows, nose, lips and ear.

DEPENDABLE SURVIVOR MALE 3

4

Draw his shirt and uniform.

5

Finally, delete all unnecessary lines
to merge the body.

111

DREAMER SURVIVOR FEMALE 2

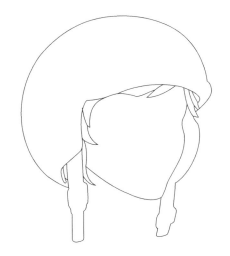

**Draw the shape of her
head with helmet and hairstyle.**

**Continue with his neck,
Solder and details of cap and hair.**

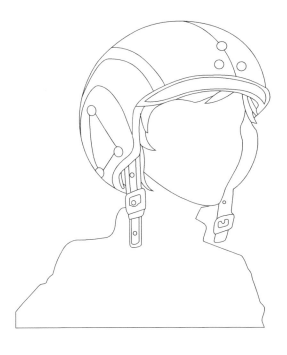

**Draw eyes, eyebrows, nose,
ear and lips.**

112

DREAMER SURVIVOR FEMALE 2

Draw her uniform with collar.

Finally, delete all unnecessary lines to merge the body.

DREAMER SURVIVOR MALE 3

**Draw the shape of
his head with hairstyle and beard.**

**Continue with her neck,
arms and details line for hair.**

**Draw eyes, eyebrows, nose and lips.
Draw his mustang.**

DREAMER SURVIVOR MALE 3

④

Draw his shirt and sweater.

⑤

Finally, delete all unnecessary lines
to merge the body.

HUSK PITCHER SURVIVOR

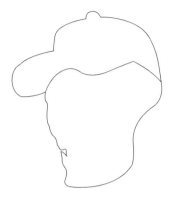

Draw the shape of His head with cap.

Continue with his neck, arms, figures and details on cap.

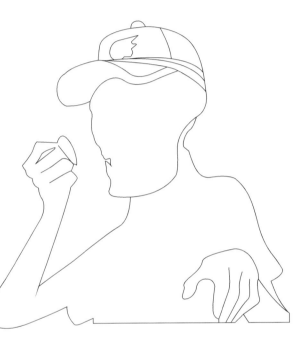

Draw eyes, eyebrows, nose and teeth.

HUSK PITCHER SURVIVOR

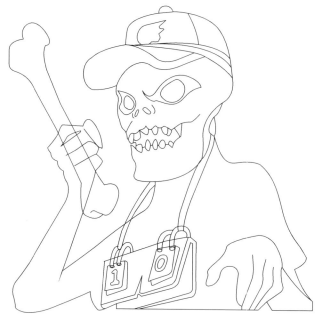

Draw bone in his hand and the calendar hanging from his neck.

Draw details of his cloth and the head mask hanging behind his neck.

5

Finally, delete all unnecessary lines to merge the body.

117

JOEL SURVIVOR

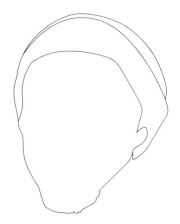

Draw the shape of
his head with cap.

Continue with his neck,
Solder and details of cap.

Draw eyes, eyebrows, nose,
ear, lips, beard and mustage.

118

JOEL SURVIVOR

④

Draw his shirt with collar.

⑤

Finally, delete all unnecessary lines to merge the body.

PRAGMATIC SURVIVOR MALE 3

**Draw the shape of
his head with mask shape and hairstyle.**

**Continue with his neck,
arms and details line for hair and lace.**

**Draw eyes, eyebrows, nose and lips.
Draw hiss armpit and other lace.**

PRAGMATIC SURVIVOR MALE 3

4 Draw his mask completely with details.

5 Now, draw his jackate and bag.

6 Finally, delete all unnecessary lines to merge the body.

121

How To Draw Fortnite For Kids: 10 Defenders, 10 Lead Survivors

FEMALE GUNSLINGER DEFENDER

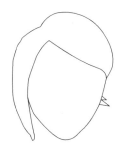

**Draw the shape of
her head with cap and hair.**

**Continue with her neck,
Solder, arm and details of the hair.**

Draw eyebrows, nose, and lips.

123

FEMALE GUNSLINGER DEFENDER

Draw her shirt with maflar.

Draw her sunglasses and belt on the arm.

Finally, delete all unnecessary lines to merge the body.

FEMALE RIFLEMAN DEFENDER

**Draw the shape of
her head with cap.**

**Continue with her neck, solder, arm
and details of cap and a chest line.**

**Draw eyes, eyebrows, nose,
ear and lips.**

FEMALE RIFLEMAN DEFENDER

Draw her uniform.

Draw her bluetooth headset, tag and knife on left arm.

5

Finally, delete all unnecessary lines to merge the body.

FEMALE SHOTGUNNER DEFENDER

**Draw the shape of
her head with cap and hair.**

**Continue with her neck, Solder, arm
and details of cap and hair. Also, the chest line.**

**Draw eyes, eyebrows, nose,
ear and lips.**

FEMALE SHOTGUNNER DEFENDER

Draw her hoodie with collar.

5

Finally, delete all unnecessary lines to merge the body.

128

FEMALE SNIPER DEFENDER

**Draw the shape of
her head with hairstyle.**

**Continue with her neck,
Solder, arm and details of the hair.**

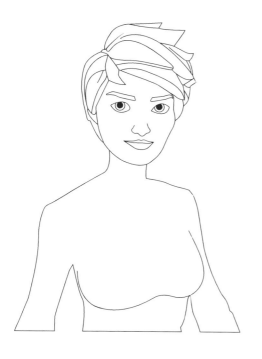

**Draw eyes, eyebrows, nose,
ear and lips.**

129

FEMALE SNIPER DEFENDER

(4) Draw her shirt with collar.

(5) Finally, delete all unnecessary lines to merge the body.

HAMLET MCKINNEY SURVIVOR

**Draw the shape of
his head with the hair.**

**Continue with his neck,
Solder and details of the hair.**

**Draw eyes, eyebrows, nose,
ear, teeths and lips.**

131

HAMLET MCKINNEY SURVIVOR

4

Draw his t-shirt and both hand.

5

Draw the switch in his right hand and the device in his left hand.

5

Finally, delete all unnecessary lines to merge the body.

132

INVENTOR FEMALE SURVIVOR

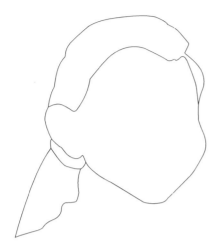

Draw the shape of her head with the hair.

Continue with his neck, Solder, hair band and details of the hair.

3

Draw eyes, eyebrows, nose, ear and lips.

INVENTOR FEMALE SURVIVOR

Draw her ear ring and glasses.

Draw her dresses with collar.

Finally, delete all unnecessary lines to merge the body.

134

LACEY CHAOS SURVIVOR

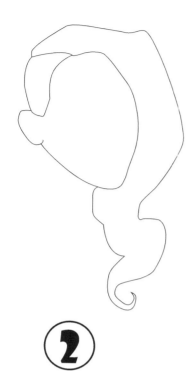

**Draw the shape of
her head with the hair.**

**Continue with his neck,
Solder, hand and details of the hair.**

**Draw eyes, eyebrows, nose,
ear and lips.**

135

LACEY CHAOS SURVIVOR

Draw lines for her dress and gloves.

Draw the rifle.

Finally, delete all unnecessary lines to merge the body.

LARA JONES SURVIVOR

**Draw the shape of
her head with the hair.**

**Continue with her neck,
Solder, hand and details of the hair.**

**Draw eyes, eyebrows, nose,
ear and lips.**

137

LARA JONES SURVIVOR

Draw the collar of her t-shirt.

Draw the rope on her left solder and in the finger.

Finally, delete all unnecessary lines to merge the body.

MALE BRUISER DEFENDER

**Draw the shape of
his head with cap and beard.**

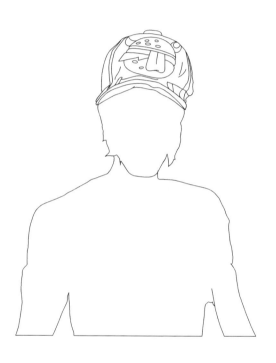

**Continue with his neck, solder,
arm and draw the details of the cap.**

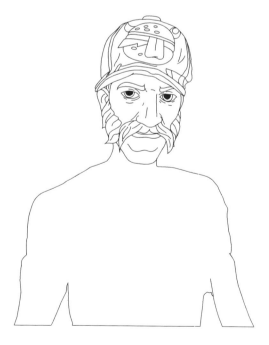

**Draw eyes, eyebrows, nose,
ear, mustage, beard details and lips.**

MALE BRUISER DEFENDER

**Draw his shirt and collar with details.
Draw the pen.**

**Finally, delete all unnecessary lines
to merge the body.**

MALE GUNSLINGER DEFENDER

**Draw the shape of
his head with cap and hair.**

**Continue with his neck,
Solder, arm and details of the hair.**

3

**Draw eyes, eyebrows, nose,
ear, beard and lips.**

141

MALE GUNSLINGER DEFENDER

Draw his shirt with collar.

Finally, delete all unnecessary lines
to merge the body.

MALE RIFLEMAN DEFENDER

**Draw the shape of
his head with cap and hair.**

**Continue with his neck,
Solder, arm and details of helmet and hair.**

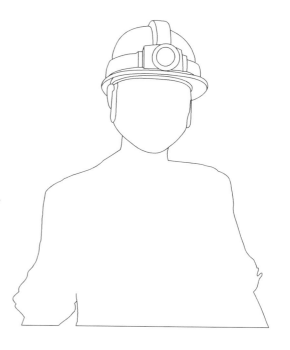

**Draw eyes, eyebrows, nose,
ear, mustang and lips.**

143

MALE RIFLEMAN DEFENDER

(4) Draw his shirt with collar.

(5) Draw his glasses.

(5) Finally, delete all unnecessary lines to merge the body.

144

MALE SHOTGUNNER DEFENDER

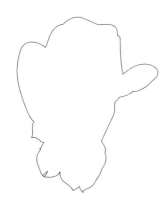

**Draw the shape of
his head with cap, hair, and beard.**

**Continue with his neck,
Solder and details of cap and hair.**

**Draw eyes, eyebrows, nose,
ear, lips, and details for beard.**

145

MALE SHOTGUNNER DEFENDER

Draw his shirt and jacket.

Draw the headphone with the wire.

⑤

Finally, delete all unnecessary lines to merge the body.

146

MALE SNIPER DEFENDER

**Draw the shape of
his head with the hair and beard.**

**Continue with his neck,
Solder, arm and details of the hair.**

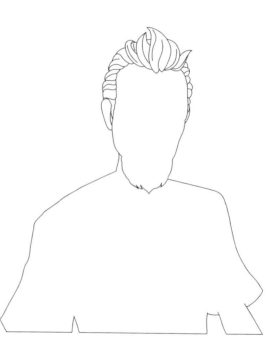

**Draw eyes, eyebrows, nose,
ear, lips, and beard.**

147

MALE SNIPER DEFENDER

Draw his shirt with tie.

Draw the glasses.

Finally, delete all unnecessary lines to merge the body.

MARTY KINGSLY SURVIVOR

Draw the shape of
his head with with the hair.

2

Continue with his neck, and Solder.

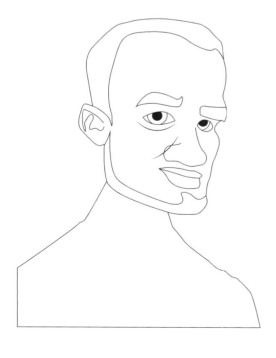

3

Draw eyes, eyebrows, nose,
ear, lips and beard.

MARTY KINGSLY SURVIVOR

4
Draw his suit and tie.

5
Finally, delete all unnecessary lines to merge the body.

NEIL KEPLER SURVIVOR

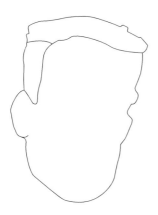

Draw the shape of his head with hair.

Draw his neck, shape of the astronaut suit and details of the hair.

Draw eyes, eyebrows, nose, ear and lips.

151

NEIL KEPLER SURVIVOR

4

Draw collar and details of the suit.

5

Finally, delete all unnecessary lines to merge the body.

NICK GOLUB SURVIVOR

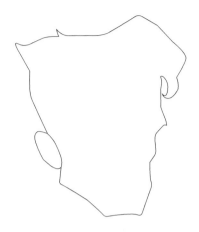

Draw the shape of his head with the hair.

Continue with his neck, Solder and details of the hair. Draw the French cut mustache too.

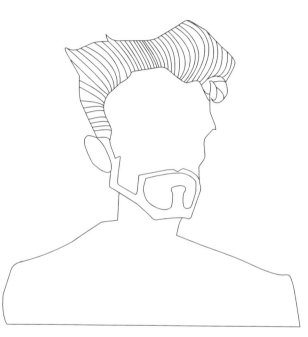

Draw eyes, eyebrows, nose, ear and lips.

153

NICK GOLUB SURVIVOR

4

Draw his suit with the collar.

5

Finally, delete all unnecessary lines to merge the body.

154

SIE LUNG SURVIVOR

**Draw the shape of
his head with the hair.**

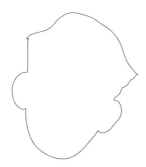

**Continue with his neck,
Solder, arm and details of the hair.**

**Draw eyes, eyebrows, nose,
ear and lips.**

155

SIE LUNG SURVIVOR

Draw his shirt with collar and lines on the fingure.

Finally, delete all unnecessary lines to merge the body.

SOLDIER FEMALE SURVIVOR

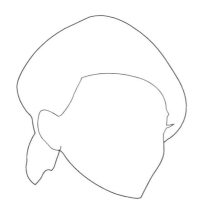

**Draw the shape of
his head with cap and hair.**

**Continue with his neck,
Solder and details of cap and hair.**

**Draw her eyes, eyebrows, nose,
ear and lips.**

157

SOLDIER FEMALE SURVIVOR

 Draw her uniform with the maflar.

 Draw the bluetooth headset.

 Finally, delete all unnecessary lines to merge the body.

TESSA LACE SURVIVOR

Draw the shape of
her head with the hair.

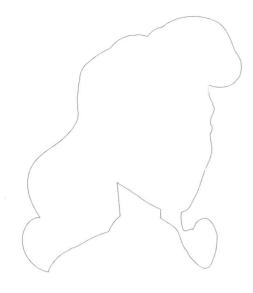

Continue with her neck,
Solder, details of the hair
and the pencil.

Draw eyes, nose,
ear and lips.

159

TESSA LACE SURVIVOR

Draw her shirt with collar.

Draw the Glasses and top
part of the eyebrows.

Finally, delete all unnecessary lines
to merge the body.

160

VAL BRUISER DEFENDER

**Draw the shape of
her head with cap.**

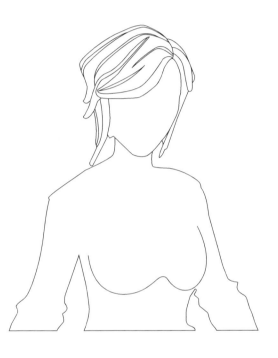

**Continue with her neck, solder, arm
and details of cap and a chest line.**

**Draw eyes, eyebrows, nose,
ear and lips.**

161

VAL BRUISER DEFENDER

Draw her uniform.

Draw the tag and knife on the left arm.

Finally, delete all unnecessary lines to merge the body.

162

Made in the USA
San Bernardino, CA
13 November 2018